D1219479

PRESIDENTIAL LOSERS

DAVID J. GOLDMAN

↳ LERNER PUBLICATIONS COMPANY • MINNEAPOLIS

Lerner Publications Company
A division of Lerner Publishing Group
241 First Avenue North
Minneapolis, MN 55401 U.S.A.

Website address: www.lernerbooks.com

Library of Congress Cataloging-in-Publication Data

Goldman, David J.
    Presidential losers / by David J. Goldman.
      p. cm.
    Summary: Highlights the political careers of a variety of candidates who lost their elections to the nation's highest office, including three-time presidential loser Henry Clay and Al Gore, who was defeated in the 2000 election after winning the popular vote. Includes bibliographical references and index.
    ISBN: 0–8225–0100–7 (lib. bdg. : alk. paper)
    1. Presidents—United States—Election—History—Juvenile literature.
2. Presidential candidates—United States—Biography—Juvenile literature.
3. Presidential candidates—United States—History—Juvenile literature.
4. United States—Politics and government—Juvenile literature. [1. Presidential candidates. 2. United States—Politics and government.] I. Title.
E176.1. G634 2004
973'.09'9—dc21   2003011222

Manufactured in the United States of America
1 2 3 4 5 6 – DP – 09 08 07 06 05 04

CONTENTS

AARON BURR

WILLIAM JENNINGS BRYAN

HENRY CLAY

ALFRED LANDON

ALBERT GORE

GEORGE MCCLELLAN

HUBERT H. HUMPHREY

ADLAI STEVENSON

SAMUEL TILDEN

THOMAS E. DEWEY

PREFACE

The first presidential losers I selected for this book were those who ran at least twice without success: Henry Clay, William Jennings Bryan, Thomas E. Dewey, and Adlai Stevenson. I then chose losers who probably should have won: Samuel Tilden and perhaps Albert Gore, as examples of the irony, complexity, and occasional unfairness of the electoral process. Three men who ran at particularly meaningful times in the nation's history were also selected: George B. McClellan, Alfred M. Landon, and Hubert Humphrey. Also, I included a loser whose story is especially interesting: Aaron Burr.

David J. Goldman
Minneapolis, MN

WHO ELECTS THE PRESIDENT?

We say "the majority rules" in the United States. The candidate most of the people vote for wins the presidency. But this is not always true. Someday you might vote for a man or a woman who gets most of the votes of the people but does not become president. This has happened in the United States four times—most recently in 2000—but it could happen in any presidential election.

How can the person who gets the most votes not be president? The answer to this question lies in the complicated way we select the president. The American people do not really elect the president. The Electoral College does.

The Electoral College is not a school but a group of men and women who never meet together. They actually vote for the president after the popular election is held. When you vote for a presidential candidate, you are really just choosing a set of electors. If you vote for the candidate from the Republican Party, you are saying, "I want the electors from the Republican Party, not the Democratic Party or any other party, to be in the Electoral College from my state." If the Republican candidate wins a majority of the votes in your state, the Republican set of electors votes for president. Electors mail their votes to Washington, D.C., where they are counted in front of both parts of Congress (the House and the Senate).

The electoral system was set up by the Constitution of the United States. The number of electors a state has is equal to the number of senators and representatives that state has in the U.S. Congress. Every state has two senators and at least one representative. States with large populations have more representatives than states with small populations. For example, California has fifty-two representatives, and North Dakota has one. California has fifty-four electoral votes, and North Dakota has only three.

If no candidate gets a majority in the Electoral College, the House of Representatives is given the job of choosing the president. The representatives from each state meet in January to decide the election. Each state gets only one vote. The House had to decide the results of the presidential election in 1800 and 1824. In 1876 it decided the outcome by delegating the decision to a special commission. The U.S. Supreme Court settled the issue in 2000.

Someday you might vote for a person who gets the majority of votes in your state, but the electors from your state do not vote for that person in the Electoral College. This can happen because in about half the states the electors can vote for any person they want to, whether that candidate wins in their state or not. Fortunately, the electors usually vote the way the majority voted.

Some voters felt that the 2000 presidential election was flawed because of the controversy over the methods used to decide the eventual winner, George W. Bush.

SO FAR, THERE HAVE BEEN NO SERIOUS ATTEMPTS

to reform or eliminate the Electoral College. But every close election shows there are some problems with the system. As in 2000, a winner of the most votes may not be elected president. This seems unfair and undemocratic to many. The Electoral College favors the voters in small, usually southern and western states. In recent years, this has benefited the Republican Party. Defenders of the Electoral College system claim that a straight popular vote would diminish the power of individual states. They say a candidate would not campaign in smaller states, concentrating instead in the major urban population areas. The debate goes on.

Many people would like to eliminate the Electoral College and have the people choose the president directly. This might well happen in your lifetime. If it does, elections will be less complicated. But they may be less interesting. As this book will show, having the Electoral College choose the president sometimes leads to unexpected results.

Since the birth of the nation, there have been fifty-four presidential elections. (The fifty-fifth takes place in November 2004.) Some of the losers were later elected president. Some became famous even though they never were president. Others were rarely heard from again. Whatever happened to them in later years, these people all shared a common bond: they had the privilege of running for the nation's highest office. That is honor enough for most people.

AARON BURR
(1756—1836)

THE ELECTION OF 1800

In the first two presidential elections of 1789 and 1792, George Washington, the hero of the Revolutionary War, was the winner. In those days, each elector voted for two names. Washington was chosen by all the electors. The person with the second largest total became vice president. Thus John Adams served for two terms as vice president. In 1796 Adams was elected president, and Thomas Jefferson, the second-place finisher, became vice president. In 1800 the contest was again between Adams and Jefferson. Aaron Burr was to make things difficult.

Aaron Burr was the most unusual of all the presidential losers. He tried to trick his party into electing him president—and he almost succeeded. All his life, Burr was a power-hungry man. He did not care how he attained power, as long as he got it.

Burr was a leading member of the Anti-Federalist Party in New York State. This party, led nationally by Thomas Jefferson, was formed to oppose the Federalists, who were led by Alexander Hamilton. These were the first political parties in the United States. The Federalists thought that only rich and well-educated people were capable of governing. They wanted the federal government to be very powerful. The Anti-Federalists believed that the common people should have a say in the government. They also wanted the states to have as much power as the federal government.

THE ANTI-FEDERALISTS WERE ACTUALLY THE forerunners of the Democratic Party. Eventually, the Federalists became known as "Whigs" and disappeared. The Republican Party began in the 1840s essentially to further the abolition of slavery.

Burr got his chance for the presidency in the election of 1800. The Anti-Federalists decided that Jefferson should run for president and Burr for vice president. Jefferson was from Virginia, so he would get votes from the southern states. Burr was from New York, so the northern states would support him. Burr agreed to run for vice president, but he knew that it was an office without much influence or power. He began to make secret plans to have himself elected president instead of Jefferson.

What Burr tried to do is impossible in modern times because the rules for electing a president have changed. Until 1804 every candidate for president or vice president ran by himself. There were no "tickets." Each elector voted for two men separately. The man who got the most votes was president, and the man who came in second was vice president. If there was a tie, the House of Representatives chose the president. Burr decided that he would try to make the election a tie in the Electoral College. He had as many friends in the House as Jefferson and thought he could win the presidency there.

The Anti-Federalists asked Burr to make sure that one or two of their electors voted for Jefferson but not for Burr. That would put Jefferson in as president with Burr as vice president. Burr agreed but secretly did nothing. When the results came in, they were just what Burr had planned. All the electors who voted for Jefferson also voted for Burr. The vote in the Electoral College was tied seventy-three to seventy-three. Burr, who was supposed to be vice president, was almost president.

The House of Representatives was asked to choose between Jefferson and Burr. In 1800 there were more Federalists in the House than Anti-Federalists. Although the Federalists themselves had lost the election, they had to decide who would be the next president. Burr probably could have stepped aside and let Jefferson be president. After all, he had been nominated only for vice president. Burr refused to do so.

With the election of 1800 in a tie, the House of Representatives made the final decision as to who would be president. The House chose Thomas Jefferson *(above)* over Aaron Burr.

This was the first election in the nation's history in which the House of Representatives had to decide the winner. The Constitution says that when an election goes to the House, each state gets one vote. Thus the representatives from each state get together in a group to vote. The candidate who wins in that state gets the state's one vote. In the election of 1800, there were only sixteen states. The candidate who received nine votes would win.

When the House met to choose the president, Jefferson got eight votes on the first ballot, and Burr got six. Two states, Vermont and Maryland, did not vote for either man. Jefferson needed one more vote to win. Burr needed three. Over a period of a week, the House voted thirty-five times, and each time the results were the same—eight for Jefferson, six for Burr, and two undecided.

The Federalists realized that they had to come to a decision. Alexander Hamilton, as the Federalist leader, had to choose between his two enemies, Jefferson and Burr. He hated Jefferson and his party, but he was afraid of Aaron Burr. He believed that Burr was a dishonest man who was more interested in power than in serving his country. Hamilton was also jealous of Burr's power in his home state of New York. So he persuaded his friends in the House to vote for Jefferson. On the thirty-sixth ballot, the votes from Vermont and Maryland went to Jefferson. Jefferson was elected president, and Burr became vice president.

Alexander Hamilton was the leader of the Federalist Party, which favored a strong central government.

While the voting was going on, Burr kept silent. If he had promised to work for the Federalist ideas, he might have swung the vote to his side. Instead, he did nothing, realizing that he would be finished with the Anti-Federalists if he made any kind of deal. Burr accepted the office of vice president, but he never forgave Hamilton for helping Jefferson to become president.

In the next four years, Burr served as a fair and dignified vice president. But he had made many political enemies. President Jefferson was unfriendly to him because he was sure that Burr had tried to trick him. Burr and Hamilton grew to hate each other. They called each other names in public, in letters, and in the newspapers. Their attacks became more and more vicious and personal. Hamilton called Burr "a dangerous man" and accused him of planning to overthrow the government. In 1804, his last year as vice president, Burr ran for governor of New York.

The bad feelings between Hamilton and Burr became greater when Burr lost the election to the man Hamilton supported.

Finally, Burr became uncontrollably angry. He challenged Hamilton to a duel in July 1804. The two men met early one morning in an empty field near Weehawken, New Jersey. Pistols were chosen as the weapons. Burr and Hamilton walked away from each other, turned, and fired. Burr proved to be the better shot, and he badly wounded Hamilton. The next day Hamilton died.

The country was shocked. The vice president had killed one of the nation's first great leaders. Burr finished his term of office, but he was no longer a popular man. Realizing that he could never be president, he began to look for another way to gain power. He traveled in the south and southwest and started making mysterious plans. Historians believe that Burr may have planned to capture Mexico and make a kingdom for himself. Or he may have plotted a rebellion of the western states against

In the early 1800s, dueling—combat between two armed persons—was considered an honorable way for wealthy gentlemen to settle certain disputes. Aaron Burr *(second from left)* challenged Alexander Hamilton *(far right)* to a duel in 1804. Hamilton died as a result. By the mid-1800s, dueling had largely been outlawed.

the eastern states. A third possibility is that Burr hoped to take over some land between Louisiana and Mexico (what would become Texas).

In the summer of 1806, Burr and sixty men began a trip down the Ohio and Mississippi Rivers in thirteen flatboats. Whatever his plans were, Burr was never able to carry them out. One of his coplotters, General James Wilkinson, betrayed Burr. He sent a letter to President Jefferson, telling him that Burr was going to attack New Orleans, Louisiana, on his way to Mexico. Burr tried to flee but was caught in South Carolina. The president had Burr arrested and charged with treason.

General James Wilkinson plotted with and then betrayed Burr, who was scheming against the U.S. government.

Burr was tried in Richmond, Virginia, in March 1807 with Supreme Court chief justice John Marshall serving as judge. The trial caused a great stir of excitement. Burr was found not guilty and set free because there was no evidence that he had done anything against the government. Most Americans, however, still believed that Burr was a traitor. After the trial, Burr went to France to seek the help of Napoleon, the French emperor, in capturing land in America. When this failed, Burr returned to New York to practice law again. He lived there for nearly twenty years but never returned to public life.

AS A RESULT OF THE ELECTION OF 1800, THE

Twelfth Amendment to the Constitution was passed in 1804. It provided that electors cast separate ballots for president and vice president.

HENRY CLAY

(1777—1852)

THE ELECTIONS OF 1824, 1832, AND 1844

Henry Clay's career in public life spanned nearly fifty years. During that time, he did everything he could to become president but never succeeded. He ran for the presidency in 1824, 1832, and 1844, and each time he was defeated. Clay was the first three-time presidential loser. (Only one other man, William Jennings Bryan, ran and lost three times.)

Henry Clay was an ambitious young man growing up in Kentucky. He began to practice law when he was twenty years old. At the age of twenty-six, he was elected to the Kentucky state legislature. His fellow legislators liked him and chose him, even though he was not yet thirty, to go to the U.S. Senate to fill out an unexpired Senate term. Although the

Constitution requires senators to be thirty years old, no one seems to have investigated his age. In any event, he was reelected to the Senate in 1809.

Clay had a powerful personality. He was a ladies' man, a storyteller, a poker player, and a drinker. He quickly became one of the most important men in Washington, D.C. However, he decided to give up his Senate seat to serve in the House of Representatives. In 1811, after Clay had been in Washington less than five years, he was elected to the House of Representatives and immediately made Speaker of the House. The Speaker runs the House and is one of the most powerful people in the federal government.

In 1816 Clay used his power to help James Monroe win the presidency. For his efforts, Clay hoped to be named secretary of state. He was sure that if he could be secretary of state, he would then be elected president. Thomas Jefferson, James Madison, and Monroe had each been secretary of state before becoming president. But Monroe gave the job to John Quincy Adams. Clay was very disappointed and used his power to make things difficult for President Monroe. For example, he did not let President Monroe take the oath of office inside the U.S. Capitol Building and refused to attend the ceremony. Clay never forgave people who crossed him.

Clay ran for the presidency for the first time in 1824, but he came in last in a four-man race. That year no candidate won a majority of votes in the Electoral College. The leading candidates were Andrew Jackson of Tennessee, who received ninety-nine votes, and John Quincy Adams of Massachusetts, who received eighty-four. William Crawford had forty-one, and Clay had only thirty-seven.

Even though Clay got the least number of votes, he came close to winning the presidency. The Constitution says that when no candidate wins an election, the House of Representatives must vote on the *three* candidates with the most votes. If Clay had received five more electoral votes, he would have come in third. Then he would have been considered for the presidency along with Jackson and Adams. And he could likely have won in the House because he was so popular there.

Clay's popularity in the House did mean that he had the power to decide which man would be president. Clay did not consider Crawford because he had a serious illness. Andrew Jackson had received the largest number of popular votes. But Clay did not want him to win. Jackson, like Clay, was from the western United States. Clay hoped to end Jackson's political career in 1824, so that Clay would have the full support of the region the next time he ran for president. However, Clay did not really like Adams either. He had not forgotten that Monroe had chosen Adams to be secretary of state instead of Clay. Clay finally decided to throw his strength to Adams, who was thus elected.

President Adams, in turn, made Clay his secretary of state. Many people, especially Jackson and his supporters, were angry with Clay. They charged that Adams had won because he and Clay had made a "corrupt bargain." Clay served as secretary of state for four years, but the job did not please him. He retired from public life when Jackson became president in the election of 1828. But Clay still hoped to be president. He did not stay out of politics for long. Clay went back to Washington as a senator in 1831.

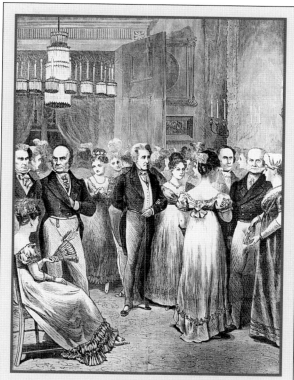

As president, John Quincy Adams held a reception for Senator Andrew Jackson, whom Adams had narrowly defeated in the election of 1824. Adams, who had won with Henry Clay's support, made Clay his secretary of state.

The next year, Clay was chosen by the Whig Party (formerly the Federalist Party) to run for president. Both the Whigs and the Democrats (formerly the Anti-Federalists) held nominating conventions in 1832. This was the first time that members of each party met together to choose the people they wanted to run for president and vice president. The Democrats

Henry Clay was a gifted speaker, who enthralled his fellow senators during debates on the Senate floor.

chose Andrew Jackson to run for a second term. Clay was a charming and powerful candidate, but the people loved Jackson, and he easily won the election. Jackson received 219 votes in the Electoral College. Clay had only 49.

After his second presidential defeat, Clay returned to the Senate, where he was still highly respected. Despite his popularity and power, Clay became increasingly bitter. He was angry about his two defeats for the presidency. He wanted to run again in 1840. But the Whigs decided that Clay could not win, and they chose another man, William Henry Harrison. Clay was asked to be the vice-presidential candidate, but he refused. Harrison won the election and died one month after taking office. This was the first of two times that Clay turned down the nomination for vice president. (The second time was in 1848 when Zachary Taylor was the party's nominee. Both times the Whigs won the election. Both times the man who was elected president died in office, and thus Clay would have become president at last.)

Clay did not give up his desire for the presidency, although his party did not nominate him in 1840. He still had great power in the Whig Party, and he gained the nomination for himself in 1844. He was sixty-seven years old, but he ran for the office with energy. Once again, he was defeated. This time, he lost to James K. Polk, the first presidential "dark horse." Polk was called a dark horse because he was not nationally known and had not been considered for the nomination until his party's convention had already started.

Clay served his country for many years, but never as its president. Few men in history have held as much power in Congress as Clay. In 1957 the U.S. Senate voted Clay one of the five greatest senators in its history. It is a fitting tribute to one of the dominant politicians of the nineteenth century.

A banner features a portrait of Clay during his third bid for the presidency in 1844. He lost to James K. Polk.

CLAY'S SPIRIT SEEMED TO FADE AFTER HIS THIRD

defeat. But he was too much a fighter to stay away from politics. He returned to the Senate in 1849 and stayed there until he died in 1852. Clay is remembered as the Great Compromiser. After the 1820s, the United States began to be divided, the North against the South, over the question of slavery. Three times between 1820 and 1850, Clay worked out plans to help the North and the South settle their differences without war. Partly because of Clay's work, the Civil War (1861–1865) was not fought in his lifetime. Unfortunately, it could not be avoided forever.

GEORGE B. McCLELLAN

(1826—1885)

THE ELECTION OF 1864

Many generals have run for the presidency. George Washington, Andrew Jackson, Zachary Taylor, Ulysses S. Grant, and Dwight D. Eisenhower were generals who later became presidents. They had become famous and respected by serving the United States in times of war. Other well-known generals—like George B. McClellan—ran for president and lost. But McClellan's story is unusual. He was not a successful general. He had been fired from his job two years before the presidential election.

In 1861, when the Civil War broke out between the Union (Northern states) and the Confederacy (Southern states), McClellan was made a major general in the Union army and was given command of the Ohio area. At first, he was a successful military leader, perhaps because he did not have to fight against very large armies. He defended Ohio and drove the Confederate forces out of western Virginia. McClellan was one of only a few Northern generals who won any battles in 1861.

McClellan's victories on the western front brought him to the attention of President Abraham Lincoln. In August 1861, Lincoln gave McClellan command of the Army of the Potomac, which had been badly defeated in its first battles. The soldiers were discouraged and not properly trained for fighting. McClellan took over and created one of the best trained and equipped armies in the world. His soldiers trusted and respected their leader.

McClellan loved to parade his troops through the streets of Washington but was reluctant to lead them into battle, no matter how well trained or equipped.

In November 1861, Lincoln appointed McClellan commander of the entire Union army. McClellan believed that he had been called to save the Union from destruction. He was convinced that he was a great soldier and the only man who would be able to win the war for the North. He read everything he could about Napoleon and sometimes believed that he was like the French emperor. Both men were short and stocky. The newspapers often called McClellan the Young

During the Civil War (1861–1865), President Lincoln *(left)* **conferred with General McClellan** *(right)*.

Napoleon. McClellan thought that his early victories in Ohio and western Virginia proved him a great general. Just as Napoleon had saved France, McClellan thought he would save America.

It was true that McClellan was very good at organizing and training soldiers. But he was reluctant to use the army. He was too cautious and fearful to attack the Confederate army. And the Young Napoleon could not be made to lead his men into battle when they did fight. Many times he was far behind the lines when the firing began. Once he slept right through a battle. He was also a very difficult man, who argued constantly with the other generals. Lincoln could not make him listen to his orders and advice. Finally, in March 1862, Lincoln removed McClellan from command of the Union forces, leaving him in charge of only the Army of the Potomac.

McClellan became very discouraged in his new position. He was afraid that he would not be able to win the war. But he received a second chance. After the Union forces were badly defeated again, President Lincoln asked McClellan to become commander of the entire army once more. The Union forces in both the eastern and the western areas were not doing well. Lincoln chose McClellan because none of the other Northern generals were any more successful than he had been.

General McClellan's performance was better the second time. The Southern forces, under General Robert E. Lee, were moving into the North. Even the city of Washington was in danger. In an enormously bloody battle, McClellan stopped the invasion of Lee's army at Antietam Creek in Maryland in September 1862. The Young Napoleon had finally won a victory. However, if a more aggressive general had been in McClellan's place, the Civil War might have been over at the Battle of Antietam. Military experts say that McClellan should have attacked Lee's soldiers as they retreated. But McClellan grew timid again. He was satisfied when he saw the Southern army leave.

President Lincoln was very unhappy with McClellan. He wanted to win the war, not just defend the city of Washington. Lincoln asked McClellan to move south to fight the Confederates. McClellan put off

More than 25,000 soldiers—both Union and Confederate—died during the Battle of Antietam.

starting for a month. Once again, in November 1862, Lincoln dismissed McClellan. The president said, "He has got the slows." It was not until July 1863 in Pennsylvania that the Union won the decisive Battle of Gettysburg, stopping the Confederate advance.

McClellan was furious with President Lincoln for his dismissal. He thought that he was a great general. Further, he disagreed when Lincoln moved to free the slaves. McClellan wanted to save the Union, but he also wanted to bring back the Southern states. He would do it all alone, if necessary. If he could not save the nation as a general, he would save it by becoming president.

McClellan began to attack President Lincoln personally. He called him "a well-meaning baboon" and "the original gorilla." The Democrats decided that the thirty-eight-year-old general would be a good candidate to run against Lincoln for the presidency in 1864. They felt that people were tired of the bloody war and that President Lincoln was becoming less popular. The general was nominated by the Democrats at their convention in

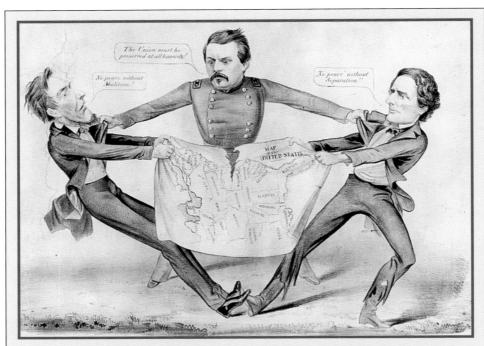

A political cartoon shows McClellan trying to keep the North and the South together. Near the end of the Civil War, McClellan ran for president because he was convinced he could save the Union.

Chicago, Illinois. McClellan was liked by many voters, and even Lincoln said that he did not see how McClellan could be beaten.

Fortunately for Lincoln, the war took a turn in the Union's favor. Generals Phillip Sheridan, William T. Sherman, and Ulysses S. Grant began to win the battles that McClellan had been too cautious to start. The Confederate army was in retreat by the time the election was held. President Lincoln was reelected, but he did not receive a large majority. The vote showed that many people agreed with McClellan. They believed that the little general was the right man to save the Union, even though he had not been a successful general.

After his defeat, McClellan returned to private life. He spent several years traveling in Europe and then became chief engineer for the New York City docks. From 1878 to 1881, he served as governor of New Jersey.

Throughout his life, he had many successful business interests. One of his projects was designing a subway system for New York City, but his plan was never used. During his last years, he wrote a book about his part in the Civil War. He was never able to convince the nation of the greatness he was sure he possessed. McClellan died in 1884.

PRESIDENT LINCOLN WAS ASSASSINATED IN 1865, just days after the Civil War ended. His successor, Andrew Johnson, was unpopular and was impeached in an attempt to remove him from office. By one vote, the Senate failed to convict him. He was succeeded by General Ulysses S. Grant, the true military hero of the war. He served two terms that were filled with dishonesty by people serving under him. During his term, the country suffered through Reconstruction, a difficult period when the postwar South was rebuilt.

SAMUEL TILDEN
(1814—1886)

THE ELECTION OF 1876

Samuel Tilden was elected president, but he never took office and never served. He lived in a time of great dishonesty and corruption in local, state, and national government. He was cheated out of the presidency by a political deal.

Tilden became famous by fighting against corruption in the city and state governments of New York. In the 1860s and early 1870s, New York City was run by Boss Tweed, who held great power in the city and the state and used it to make himself and his friends rich. Tweed and his men padded payrolls by adding people who did not exist and collecting their wages. They received kickbacks from contracts. Part of the money paid to a contractor would go into the pocket of the government employee who set up the contract. A particular courthouse took almost fifteen years to be

William "Boss" Tweed ran New York City in the mid-1800s.

built. Elections were fixed. Tweed paid people to vote the "right" way, and often his men used force to get votes. Sometimes election officials reported the results without even counting the ballots. Once Tweed put his man into the governorship of New York with more votes than there were voters. Even the judges in New York did what Boss Tweed told them to. Honest New Yorkers did not see any way to get rid of the Tweed machine.

After this corruption was exposed by the *New York Times*, Tilden and his followers began to work for reform and improvement of city and state politics. Their first move was to elect honest judges. Then they took Boss Tweed and his ring to court and published their crimes in newspapers. Tweed was sent to jail. The thankful citizens elected Tilden governor of New York in 1874. Then he attacked another group of political crooks, the Canal Ring. These men ran the Erie Canal (an artificial waterway connecting the Great Lakes to the Atlantic Ocean) and were also cheating the taxpayers. Tilden took care of this ring as quickly as he had the Tweed machine.

The federal government, under President Ulysses S. Grant, was also corrupt during the 1870s. Dishonest politicians and businessowners were stealing millions of dollars from the federal treasury. Two of Grant's closest advisers were involved in the theft, and they were never punished. Tilden, the great reformer, looked like the man to clean up Washington. The Democrats nominated him for the presidency in 1876. The Republican candidate was Rutherford B. Hayes.

Both parties ran dirty campaigns, a common practice in politics of the time. The Democrats talked about the dishonesty of Grant's Republican government, although sometimes in exaggeration. They reminded people of the terrible events of the Civil War, and they said that the Democrats had sided with the rebels and therefore were not loyal Americans. Many Republicans whispered that Tilden was "a drunkard, a liar, a cheat, a counterfeiter."

When the votes were counted on election day, Tilden looked like the winner. Newspapers all over the country reported that he was the nineteenth president. Tilden had beaten Hayes by a quarter of a million popular votes. But in electoral votes, Tilden had 184 and Hayes had 166. To win the election, one candidate needed 185 electoral votes. Nineteen electoral votes were still in doubt. In South Carolina, Louisiana, and Florida, both the Democrats and the Republicans claimed victory.

Banners feature the presidential options for the 1876 election: Samuel Tilden and Thomas Hendricks for the Democrats and Rutherford Hayes and William Wheeler for the Republicans.

Tilden needed just one more electoral vote to win. If Hayes received all the votes from the three states, he would win. The stalemate started the greatest political wheeling and dealing of the century. Money was sent from the northern states to help the electors make the "right" decision. Bribes and promises of good federal jobs were made to local officials. Finally, on December 6, 1876, Republican electors met in the three states and voted for Hayes. But on the same day, three sets of Democratic electors met and cast votes for Tilden.

The whole problem was sent to Congress for a decision. The U.S. Constitution is not specific about what to do when states cannot decide who has received the most votes. So a special commission was selected to decide who had really won the election. Fifteen men were chosen for the commission—five representatives, five senators, and five supreme court justices. The commission was supposed to be split evenly between the two parties—seven Republicans and seven Democrats. The fifteenth man, a judge, was supposed to be neutral, neither a Republican nor a Democrat. However, just before the commission met, the neutral judge was elected to a Senate seat in a special election. Since he was to be a senator, he was ruled out of the commission. The empty place was taken by a Republican, giving Hayes's supporters a one-vote advantage.

The commission decided, by a vote of eight to seven, that Hayes had won in South Carolina, Louisiana, and Florida. All 19 electoral votes went to Hayes, who then had 185 votes to Tilden's 184. Hayes was the new president by one electoral vote.

The Democrats were furious. At first, they refused to accept the decision. Behind the scenes, however, a deal had been made. The southern Democrats were shown that it would be good for their party if the Republican candidate became president. They were promised many special considerations. One was the removal of all U.S. Army troops that had been stationed in the southern states since the Civil War. This meant that the Republicans would no longer be in control of the southern state governments. The southern Democrats decided not to oppose Hayes and accepted the deal offered by the Hayes supporters. The northern Democrats were

DEMOCRATS 'PUT UP' OR SHUT UP

I Want to BET From $100 to $500!

THAT R. B. HAYES Will be elected President of the United States of America. The money is now deposited at the office of the HERALD AND UNION.

Nov. 6th, 1876. GEORGE MARLETTE.

Deals were made to decide the 1876 election, but many voters felt that fraud had been committed in the election process. Nevertheless, Tilden lost, and Hayes became president.

thus forced to give in also. Hayes was officially declared president just two days before he was sworn in.

The nation was shocked. The people clearly wanted Tilden. He had received a majority of the popular vote. The politicians, not the people, had decided that Hayes would be president. Tilden's party workers screamed "Robbery!" and "Rutherfraud!" They staged many parades and rallies. But Tilden refused to even comment. He remained silent and watched from a distance. Tilden feared that another civil war would break out if the election became too big an issue. Also, Tilden knew that many Democrats were no more honest than the Republicans. In the southern states, they had kept many newly freed black Americans away from the polls on election day to prevent them from voting for the Republican candidate.

Tilden accepted the politicians' decision calmly and returned to private life. Since his supporters had no leader, the excitement passed away. More than any of the presidential losers, Samuel Tilden had actually been elected.

WILLIAM JENNINGS BRYAN

(1860—1925)

THE ELECTIONS OF 1896, 1900, AND 1908

Probably the most famous of all presidential losers is William Jennings Bryan. He is the only other three-time loser besides Henry Clay and the first one from the Democratic Party. Bryan ran for the presidency in 1896, 1900, and 1908. He was popular because he seemed very much like an average American. In fact, many people called him the Commoner. Bryan was considered the greatest public speaker of his time.

Bryan's favorite cause was "free-silver" coinage. He wanted the government to use more silver for money. In 1873 the United States had gone on the gold standard. Gold, not silver, was used to back paper money and make dollar coins. This meant that the amount of money available to the people was limited by the amount of gold in the U.S. Treasury. In 1878 the treasury began buying some silver and using it for dollars, but the amount of silver it could buy was limited by law. Thus there still was not much money available in the 1880s and 1890s. Bryan believed that free-silver coinage, with no limit to the amount of silver the treasury could buy, would bring more money to the common people.

The Americans who were poorest at this time were midwestern and southern farmers and workers. These were the common people that Bryan was closest to. He believed that if the government kept the gold standard, the farmers and workers would get even poorer. Free-silver coinage, Bryan believed, would bring them more money and a better living.

In 1894 Bryan ran for the U.S. Senate from Nebraska and lost. In 1896 the Democratic Party held its national convention in Chicago, Illinois. As in every convention, the delegates had to decide what causes they were going to support. The midwesterners were free-silver backers, but the Democrats from the eastern states supported the gold standard. The delegates could agree on hardly anything. Bryan was scheduled to talk on the free-silver question. He was the last of six speakers. His moment had arrived.

A banner presents William Jennings Bryan and his family. The banner commemorated Bryan's Cross of Gold speech, which won him the Democratic nomination in 1896.

He filled the hall with his mighty voice telling the delegates about the evil of the gold standard. The delegates at first sat still, as if he had cast a spell on them. Then they grew wild with excitement, roaring with approval. They cheered and yelled at every line. "You shall not press down upon the brow of labor this crown of thorns, you shall not crucify mankind upon a cross of gold!" he concluded. The Cross of Gold speech made him an instant hero to the convention.

The delegates accepted free silver, and they also found a new leader. Bryan was nominated for the presidency on the fifth ballot. He had barely been able to get a seat in the convention hall, but with one overpowering speech, he had become the Democratic candidate.

Bryan's success was really not surprising. He was a skillful speaker, but this speech was not new. In fact, Bryan had given parts of it before. He had been making speeches all over the country for three years to get people interested in the free-silver cause. Bryan knew that he could capture the delegates if he had a chance to speak. His Cross of Gold speech is one of the most famous political speeches ever given in America.

After Bryan accepted the nomination at the convention, he started a blazing campaign. He was one of the first presidential candidates to visit many distant parts of the country. He traveled more than eighteen thousand miles and gave as many as thirty-one speeches a day. Over five million people heard him speak in person. His tall, broad-shouldered frame and his large head made him a handsome figure. With his booming voice and powerful speaking style, Bryan swayed the voters.

William McKinley was the Republican running for the presidency. His campaign was managed by a clever Ohio businessman named Mark Hanna. Hanna received large gifts of money from eastern businessmen who did not want Bryan to be president. He used some of this money to bring groups of

William McKinley, the Republican candidate, opposed Bryan in the 1896 election.

people to McKinley's house. McKinley stood on his front porch and spoke to each group. But sometimes the campaign of 1896 became dirty. A favorite Republican chant was, "McKinley drinks soda water/Bryan drinks rum/McKinley is a gentleman/Bryan is a bum."

Although this rhyme was unfair, Bryan and McKinley were very different from one another. McKinley was a candidate for businessowners, rich people, and easterners. Bryan represented farmers, the southern states, and the Midwest. Bryan had great fondness for the white common people. He cared more for them than he did for issues or ideas. But Bryan could also be prejudiced and narrow minded. For example, he openly disliked black Americans. He was more a man of emotion than of reason.

McKinley won the election by a good margin—271 electoral votes to 155. Bryan's exciting speeches were not enough. Still, Bryan kept control of the Democratic Party. He wanted to run for president in the next election. During the time McKinley was president, Bryan went on speaking tours all over the country. His silver-tongued speeches still brought people out in great numbers. He continued to support free silver, and he also spoke out against American control of the Philippines after the Spanish-American War (1898). His speeches kept people from forgetting him.

In 1900 Bryan again ran for the presidency. However, by

Bryan's 1900 campaign poster. He lost for a second time.

then good times had returned to the country. Farmers and workers were not as destitute as they had been in 1896. President McKinley took advantage of the plentiful period. He campaigned on the slogan, a "Full Dinner Pail," reminding the people that good times had come while he was president. Bryan was defeated again, but he remained important in the Democratic Party. President McKinley was assassinated in 1901. He was succeeded by Theodore Roosevelt, who had been a hero in the Spanish-American War.

In 1904 Bryan did not seek the nomination for the presidency. The Democratic candidate was Alton B. Parker, a New York judge who did not support the free-silver cause. Bryan did very little to help Parker win. He quietly hoped that Theodore Roosevelt, the Republican president, would win, so that he could get the Democratic nomination for himself in 1908. His wish came true. Parker did

In the 1900 election, Bryan again ran against McKinley, who had been president for four years. A political cartoon references the view that the McKinley administration had brought prosperity to the nation in the form of a "full dinner pail."

lose the election, and four years later, the Democrats nominated Bryan to run again.

In 1908 Bryan was a presidential candidate for the third time. Unfortunately, he was no longer the dashing, exciting young thirty-six-year-old he had been in 1896. He was now forty-eight. His appearance was less attractive, and his speaking ability was starting to fade. He argued for the silver standard, for suffrage (voting rights) for women, and for a federal income tax. His moment had come and gone. William Howard Taft easily won the election for the Republicans. William Jennings Bryan never ran for president again.

Bryan could not stay out of the national spotlight, however. He used his power in the Democratic Party to get Woodrow Wilson the presidential nomination in 1912. When Wilson was elected, he chose Bryan to be his secretary of state. Bryan served until he and the president could no longer agree on what the United States should do about World War I (1914–1918), which was then being fought in Europe. Bryan was completely against war and did not want Wilson to take sides against Germany. In 1915 Bryan resigned. The United States entered the war in 1917.

William Jennings Bryan never became president, but many of the ideas he worked for—including greater use of silver, the income tax, and the vote for women—eventually came to reality. He was a man ahead of his times on some issues but ignorant and narrow on others.

THE LAST EPISODE IN BRYAN'S LIFE MADE HIM

unforgettable, but it also was embarrassing to him. In 1925 Bryan took part in the Scopes trial in Tennessee. John T. Scopes was on trial for teaching the theory of evolution. This theory says that plants and animals evolved from earlier species. Bryan and his followers could not accept the possibility that humans came from lower animals such as monkeys or apes. Bryan believed in the account of creation as stated in the Bible. This account says that humans descended only from Adam and Eve. During the 1920s, Bryan had helped to pass laws in several southern states forbidding the teaching of the theory of evolution in school.

When Scopes was brought to trial, Bryan worked to have him convicted. Clarence Darrow, a skillful lawyer, defended Scopes.

Bryan during the 1925 Scopes trial. He died that same year.

The whole country became interested in the results of the "monkey trial." Bryan's side won. Scopes was found guilty of breaking the law and fined one hundred dollars. But it really was a defeat, not a victory, for Bryan. When Darrow cross-examined him, Bryan seemed ignorant and foolish. Bryan knew almost nothing about modern science. He came out of the trial a broken man. Five days later, he died.

ALFRED LANDON

(1887—1987)

THE ELECTION OF 1936

Many men have lost presidential elections. Some have lost more than once. Most are forgotten. A few are remembered because of other accomplishments in their lives. One man, Alfred Landon, is remembered because he endured the greatest presidential defeat in U.S. history.

Landon became a Kansas oil millionaire during the 1920s. This period in American history is known as the Roaring Twenties. The country seemed very prosperous, and many people enjoyed the good times. Then in 1929, the good times suddenly ended. The stock market crashed, banks closed, many lost their homes, and businesses went bankrupt. Millions of people were out of work. Others were close to starvation. This period is called the Great Depression. Conditions grew worse, and the Republican president Herbert Hoover seemed unable to solve the nation's problems. In 1932 the American voters elected Franklin D. Roosevelt, Democratic governor of New York, to be president. In the same year, the voters of Kansas elected Republican Alf Landon to be their governor.

President Roosevelt gave the country what he called a New Deal. He created many new programs, including social security and regulation of the banking and financial industries. He began spending government money to bring back prosperity. Alf Landon kept things about the same in Kansas. He did not believe that the government should spend large amounts of money to improve economic conditions. He kept the Kansas state government from spending more money than it took in. As governor, Landon always had his door open to the people. He was happy to listen to their problems. The people of Kansas liked Landon. He operated the government like a sensible businessman. In 1934 he was the only Republican governor reelected in the whole country.

In 1936 President Roosevelt was up for reelection. The people would decide whether they liked the reform programs of the New Deal. The Republicans were hopeful of victory. They nominated the best-known man

As governor of Kansas, Landon felt the government should stay within its budget. Meanwhile, devastating dust storms blew across the state, which received federal help to recover.

in their party, Alf Landon. Landon was popular with the Kansas voters because he was able to get out and meet the people. But it was impossible for him to meet nearly 130 million Americans. Both presidential candidates had to reach the people by radio. Landon did not do well on the radio. His voice was dull, slow, and boring. President Roosevelt was the opposite. His voice came over the radio in a warm, positive, friendly manner.

Landon tried to reach the nation the same way he had reached the people of Kansas. He offered himself as a simple small-town businessman, an honest politician who was close to the people. He would balance the nation's budget and save money in government. Two of his campaign slogans were "Save the American Way of Life" and "Life, Liberty, and Landon." But his speeches, like his radio broadcasts, were uninteresting and awkward. President Roosevelt was a masterful campaigner. He was clever and quick and knew how to use his power and personality. Large crowds cheered him wherever he went.

Some political experts began to predict the election winners before the election was held. They asked a number of people how

Alf Landon and his wife waved to well-wishers after he had received the Republican Party's nomination at the 1936 convention.

they were going to vote. From this information, they predicted how all the people would vote. This is called a political poll. In the first real national use of this technique, the pollsters decided that Landon would win the election. James Farley, national chairman of the Democratic Party, predicted that Landon would lose the election. Almost no one believed him.

On election night in November 1936, Landon went to bed early. He did not need to stay up late to see who would be president. Landon was given the greatest defeat of any candidate in the history of the United States up to that time. He received only 8 electoral votes to Roosevelt's 523. He also lost by eleven million popular votes. The pollsters had been wrong. They had not asked the right people.

Landon was surprised by his smashing defeat. He continued to take part in Kansas politics but eventually retired to private life. His simple ways satisfied Kansas, but they were not enough for a nation in the middle of the Great Depression.

IN 1940 PRESIDENT ROOSEVELT RAN FOR AN

unprecedented third term. Ever since George Washington, presidents had traditionally limited themselves to two terms. Franklin Roosevelt, having led the country out of the Great Depression, was prepared to lead the country through World War II (1939–1945), which European nations were already fighting. In 1940 he defeated Wendell Willkie to win a third term. On December 7, 1941, Japan attacked the American fleet at Pearl Harbor on the Hawaiian island of Oahu. The attack decimated the fleet, and many American lives were lost. World War II had begun for America.

Between 1932 and 1944, Franklin Roosevelt won election to four terms as president. Passed in 1947, the Twenty-second Amendment to the U.S. Constitution limited presidents to two terms in office.

THOMAS E. DEWEY
(1902—1971)

YOU MUST BE AT LEAST THIS TALL TO BE ELECTED PRESIDENT!

THE ELECTIONS OF 1944 AND 1948

George Martin Dewey was one of the early leaders of the Republican Party in the 1840s. Thomas Dewey, his grandson, led that party twice in the race for the White House. Dewey was the first two-time Republican presidential loser. Even though he never became president, Dewey is remembered because of his fine record fighting crime in New York City.

Confident and well organized, Dewey expected that when he gave orders, they would be obeyed. These qualities made him an excellent crime fighter. Dewey's personality made him seem stiff and formal in public. People had a hard time feeling close to him. The same qualities that made him a good crime fighter made him a poor politician.

Dewey was short with a small mustache. He always tried to make himself look taller than he was. When photographers took a picture of him seated at his desk, he sat on a thick telephone book. He even had the ceiling in his office lowered to make him seem taller. His size, his mustache, and his formal personality led people to call him the "little man on the wedding cake."

Organized crime and its violence plagued New York City, and Dewey wanted to do something about it. He began his crime-fighting career in 1935 as prosecuting attorney for New York County. He hired the best men to help him. They set up visible offices on the fourteenth floor of the Woolworth Building in New York City. Dewey and his men were hard-working, clever, and extremely careful. They tapped phones, checked bank deposits and tax records, and got witnesses to testify. They waited until they had an unbeatable case before arresting anyone. Dewey had a nearly

Dewey and his team discuss crime fighting in front of a crowd of reporters and photographers.

perfect record of successfully prosecuting cases. In a two-year period, he won seventy-one out of seventy-three cases. Some of the nation's biggest criminals were put in prison because of Dewey's efforts.

One of the crime rings Dewey broke up involved the protection racket (an organization that uses threats to force businesses to pay it money). Criminals were making businessowners pay for "protection." People who refused to pay found their businesses damaged. If the owners complained, they were beaten or killed. Dewey brought these racketeers to trial, something no one else had been able to do. He seemed so young in appearance that the newspapers called him the "Boy Scout."

As time went on, Dewey became even better known to the American people. In 1937 he was reelected district attorney of New York County. He ran for governor of New York in 1938 but was defeated in a close election. He returned to his position as district attorney and once again began to put lawbreakers in prison. He jailed a group of criminals known as Murder, Incorporated.

Dewey ran for governor of New York again in 1942. This time he was elected. A strong-willed politician, he was able to get several good laws passed. However, many people thought that Dewey was too bossy and that he had too much control of the state legislature. His iron will as well as his cool manner kept him from being a truly popular governor.

By 1944 Dewey thought that it was time for him to run for the presidency. He was nominated by the Republicans to try to beat the country's popular three-term president Franklin Roosevelt. This was quite a job for a young man of forty-two.

At the time of the election, the United States was busy fighting World War II. Unfortunately for Dewey, Americans seemed more interested in finishing the war than in changing presidents. Dewey was in a difficult position. It would seem disloyal to attack the president. So he said that the nation needed new leaders, not "tired old men." Dewey was a sharp, crisp, and effective campaigner. But he had no real issue on which to win support. The people decided to stick with Roosevelt, and he was elected for a fourth term.

U.S. soldiers were fighting battles in Europe and the Pacific in 1944, when Dewey opposed Franklin Roosevelt in the presidential election. Roosevelt won, but his vice president, Harry Truman, finished his term.

In 1946 Dewey was reelected governor of New York, and he remained in the national spotlight. Again in 1948, he received the Republican nomination for president. This time, Harry S. Truman was the Democratic candidate. Truman had been Roosevelt's vice president and had become president after Roosevelt's death in April 1945. Although Truman had led the United States through the end of World War II, by 1948 he was not popular.

Practically everyone expected Dewey to be an easy winner against Truman. Dewey was confident of victory. He ran a well organized but unexciting campaign. He asked the voters if they had "had enough" of "Democratic" government, but he was afraid to say anything that might

Dewey, the Republican nominee again in 1948, was popular in the New York area because of his earlier crime-fighting activities.

offend anyone. It seemed as if he were just waiting out the time until the election. He was playing not to lose.

Truman was having his own troubles. He was almost the only person who thought he had a chance to win the election. Truman (nicknamed "Give 'em hell, Harry") started to fight back. He went on a long whistle-stop tour of the country. He gave short speeches from the back of a train as it stopped at the small communities on the way. He traveled nearly thirty-two thousand miles and made 356 speeches. Many people decided that they liked Truman. He seemed like "one of the folks." Dewey, on the other hand, was a "city slicker." It began to look like a closer election than the Republicans had expected.

When the polls closed on election day, almost everyone thought that Dewey had won. The early voting results showed him ahead. The newspapers were already declaring Dewey the winner. The *Chicago Daily Tribune* headline read: DEWEY DEFEATS TRUMAN. People went to bed believing that Dewey was their next president. But when they awoke, things had changed. The late results from the western states showed that President Truman was the winner by a narrow margin.

Truman holds up a paper declaring his election defeat in 1948. Many people— even some newspaper editors—thought Dewey was sure to win.

Dewey had stayed up all night, and at 5 o'clock in the morning, he said that he was "still confident." But at noon that day, he had to admit that Truman had won. Thomas Dewey became a two-time loser in one of the great upsets in presidential history.

In 1950 Dewey was elected governor of New York for a third time. When he finished that term in 1954, he retired to private life and once again became a New York lawyer until his death in 1971.

ADLAI STEVENSON
(1900—1965)

THE ELECTIONS OF 1952 AND 1956

Losing the 1944 and 1948 elections consecutively gave the Republican Party its first two-time presidential loser. The next two elections gave the Democratic Party another two-time loser, Adlai Stevenson. Probably the biggest reason for Stevenson's losses was the great popularity of the Republican candidate, General Dwight D. Eisenhower, former supreme commander of World War II Allied forces. Ike, as Eisenhower was called, was one of the most revered men in twentieth-century U.S. history.

Stevenson, too, had many qualities that gained him wide popularity. He was an excellent public speaker. His speeches were pleasant, clever, and witty. Stevenson was well educated. In fact, his opponents teasingly called him an "egghead," a reference to his intellect and cultured style. Stevenson was also well connected to U.S. politics. His grandfather, Adlai E. Stevenson, had been vice president under Grover Cleveland from 1893 to 1897 and had run as the vice-presidential candidate with William Jennings Bryan in 1900. By 1949 Stevenson was serving as governor of Illinois.

In 1952 President Truman decided not to run for reelection. His popularity was low with the American people, many of whom felt it was time for a change. The Democrats had been in the White House for twenty years, and the voters began looking for a new candidate. Truman's choice was Governor Stevenson. But Stevenson said he was not interested in the presidency. Before the convention, some party members in Illinois began a Draft Stevenson movement. This meant that they would try to get Stevenson nominated even though he had said he did not want to run. They thought that if Stevenson were chosen by the convention, he could not turn down the nomination.

Luckily for Stevenson's supporters, the 1952 Democratic convention was held in Chicago, Illinois. As governor of Illinois, Stevenson was to give the welcoming speech to the delegates. The party members were impressed with his intelligent and pleasant manner. They gave him a completely unplanned demonstration, clapping and shouting their approval. The Draft Stevenson movement grew, and other candidates began to lose strength. On the third ballot, Stevenson was nominated. Only a very few times in American history has the nomination been given to a man who said he did not want to be president.

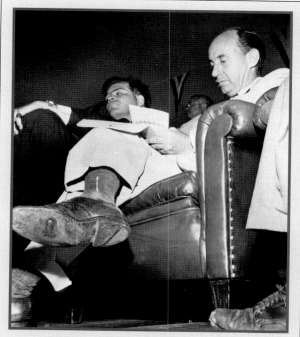

During the grueling 1952 campaign, a photographer caught the fact that even Stevenson's shoes were feeling the strain.

The Republicans knew that they had a good chance to win in 1952 if they had a well-known candidate. Their party had been out of the White House since 1932, when Franklin Roosevelt had been first elected. The Republicans asked General Eisenhower to run, and he accepted.

BOTH THE DEMOCRATS AND THE REPUBLICANS had asked Eisenhower to run as their candidate in 1948, but he had turned them down. General Eisenhower enjoyed enormous popularity as the leader of the victorious Allied armies in Europe during World War II.

Stevenson and Eisenhower staged an exciting campaign. Ike's gentle, fatherly ways appealed to the public. He had a warm, sincere personality and a friendly grin. The voters seemed to want someone who was more than just a politician. "I Like Ike" buttons were seen everywhere.

Stevenson was very popular with certain groups in the country, especially labor unions, liberals, and staff and students on college campuses. His intelligence and clever stories made him a good candidate. "Madly for Adlai" buttons were in great demand. Unfortunately, Stevenson was attacked by some people who believed it was not good for a president to be too smart or too well educated.

Ike buttons were popular during the campaign.

When the election was held, Eisenhower defeated Stevenson easily. He won by such a large margin in the Electoral College (442 to 89 votes) that it was called a landslide victory. The popular vote was closer, thirty-three million to twenty-seven million.

Stevenson was an entertaining speaker, who was at home with many segments of the voting public.

A defeated presidential candidate usually keeps great power within his party. This was true of Stevenson after 1952. He received the Democratic Party's presidential nomination again in 1956, even though many of the delegates favored Senator Estes Kefauver of Tennessee. Kefauver was famous for his investigation of organized crime. After Stevenson was nominated, the convention chose Kefauver to run for vice president.

Stevenson's campaign in 1956 was not as lively as it had been in 1952. President Eisenhower had had a heart attack during his first term, but he remained popular with the American people. The citizens trusted him, and he promised them more peace and prosperity. They felt that the country was in good hands with Eisenhower in command. Stevenson was defeated again. This time he received only 73 electoral votes to Ike's 457.

Stevenson and Kefauver, the vice-presidential nominee, acknowledged the support of the crowd at the 1956 Democratic convention.

The second defeat was enough for Stevenson. He left politics and returned to his law practice. He was put forward at the Democratic convention in 1960, as many delegates wanted to give him the nomination for a third time. Instead, Senator John F. Kennedy was nominated to be the Democratic Party candidate and was later elected.

In 1962 President Kennedy called Stevenson back to public service. He appointed Stevenson the U.S. ambassador to the United Nations (an organization of nations that works for world peace). Here was a place in which Stevenson's many talents could be properly used. He became one of the world's most respected statespeople.

Stevenson died in 1965 while on an official trip to London, England. His heart failed while he was walking in the street only a few feet from the American embassy. Stevenson's death saddened people around the world. They had come to respect the gentle and wise ways of this two-time presidential loser.

Ambassador Stevenson listens to a speech at the United Nations.

STEVENSON'S ROLE IN REPRESENTING THE UNITED

States at the UN during the Cuban Missile Crisis of 1962 was perhaps his finest hour. This crisis pitted the United States against the Soviet Union, which had secretly placed long-range missiles in Cuba. The missiles could easily reach the United States.

HUBERT H. HUMPHREY
(1911—1978)

THE ELECTION OF 1968

The assassination of President Kennedy in 1963 put his vice president, Lyndon Johnson, in office. The next year, Johnson won election to the presidency in a landslide over Senator Barry Goldwater of Arizona. Johnson selected Hubert Humphrey, the liberal senator from Minnesota, as his running mate.

From 1964 to 1968, the United States went through one of its greatest periods of upheaval, including general social and political confusion. With a huge electoral mandate, Johnson had ambitious plans. He embraced the civil rights movement, which called for an end to racial segregation and for fulfillment of equal rights for African Americans, especially in the areas of education, voting, and public accommodations.

THE CIVIL RIGHTS MOVEMENT ANGERED MANY

white voters in the southern states, where Johnson's new legislation would have the most impact. (Blacks in the southern United States had long experienced discrimination in housing, in schooling, in employment, in voting, and in everyday life.) Southern white voters had been heavy

Marchers, including Dr. Martin Luther King Jr. *(front row, far left),* **support one another during a peaceful civil rights demonstration in the 1960s.**

supporters of the Democratic Party since the Civil War, and some tried to slow Johnson's program. As Johnson was pushing the legislation through Congress, some civil rights leaders took matters to the streets and college campuses. In a series of marches, sit-ins, and demonstrations, they pursued their goals despite sometimes brutal police tactics and jail sentences. Among the most respected black leaders was Dr. Martin Luther King Jr. of Georgia.

Johnson also embarked on an expansion of U.S. involvement in the Vietnam War (1954–1975). While Presidents Eisenhower and Kennedy had tried to limit America's involvement in the civil war of this Southeast Asian country, President Johnson felt it was his duty to fight Communism in Asia. Toward this end, he dramatically increased the number of American troops stationed in South Vietnam to close to 750,000. The military draft was also increased. The war to aid South Vietnam in its strug- gle against Communist North Vietnam cost many American lives. Gradually, Americans throughout the country started demonstrating against the war in greater and greater numbers.

America's involvement in the Vietnam War (1954–1975) reached its height in the late 1960s, under President Lyndon Johnson.

Soon the demonstrators' opinions in both the antiwar and civil rights movements entered the political system. By 1967 the country had become greatly divided. Frustrated by the lack of progress on either the antiwar or civil rights fronts, demonstrators rioted in some inner-city ghettos. This was the national scene when the 1968 election rolled around.

President Johnson appeared certain of nomination by his party and of probable reelection by the country. Governors George Romney, William W. Scranton, and Nelson Rockefeller were among active Republican candidates. Another Republican candidate was former vice president Richard M. Nixon, who was practicing law in New York City. (He had lost to John F. Kennedy in the 1960 presidential race.)

NIXON'S 1960 LOSS TO JOHN F. KENNEDY WAS

one of the closest elections in history. Kennedy won the popular vote by only one hundred thousand votes out of about seventy-five million cast (about one-tenth of 1 percent). The electoral vote was not as close, 303 to 219. Nixon considered challenging the vote count but thought it was not in the nation's best interest.

Meanwhile, former Alabama governor George Wallace was making his presence felt as a viable third-party candidate. His ideas appealed especially to white southerners who wished to preserve segregation. These voters traditionally voted for the Democratic nominee. Wallace could take away votes from the Democratic Party's candidate. This would help Republicans, especially in the southern states.

Governor George Wallace *(left)* **got a warm reception from supporters during the 1968 presidential campaign. He was running as a third-party candidate.**

On the Democratic side, Senator Eugene McCarthy of Minnesota emerged as an opponent to President Johnson and his Vietnam policies. McCarthy attracted wide attention among a public disturbed by the continued loss of life in Southeast Asia. He was particularly popular among young people on college campuses. He challenged President Johnson for the Democratic Party's nomination in the New Hampshire primary (an early vote to show preference for a candidate). Because this was the earliest primary of the season, it had great symbolic meaning. Although he didn't win the primary, McCarthy came in a very strong second to Johnson. The impact was devastating to the president because it revealed the growing strength of the opposition to him and his policies within his own party.

By March 1968, the U.S. Army's losses were showing how powerful North Vietnam's forces actually were. In a startling turnabout, President Johnson announced he would not seek reelection in November but would instead concentrate on establishing peace in Vietnam. His decision was soon followed by the assassination of civil rights leader Dr. Martin Luther King Jr. Riots erupted in black sections of major cities. Some politicians, such as Senator Robert Kennedy, tried to quell rioting near the U.S. Capitol in Washington, D.C. But in Chicago, police "fired to maim" on orders of Mayor Richard J. Daley.

The conventions of the political parties were held amid this emotional

Saigon, the capital of South Vietnam, was in flames during the 1968 Tet offensive. U.S. losses during this battle convinced President Johnson not to run for reelection. This left the field open for his vice president, Hubert H. Humphrey.

Soldiers patrolled the streets of Washington, D.C., during the riots that followed the murder of Dr. Martin Luther King Jr.

upheaval. On the Republican side, Richard Nixon received the endorsement of his party in July 1968. He said he had a secret plan to end the Vietnam War. Wallace would run as the American Independent Party candidate. He promised to restore law and order to the streets of America.

The Democratic nomination seemed up for grabs, however. Senator Robert Kennedy announced his candidacy for president. Vice President Humphrey was also in line to vie for the Democratic Party's nomination. While McCarthy and Kennedy battled in primaries throughout the country, Vice President Humphrey worked to secure the commitments of Democratic Party regulars, delegates, and labor unions and did not compete in the primaries. Senators Kennedy and McCarthy engaged in a heated battle in the California primary, which Kennedy won narrowly. Tragically, however, Kennedy was assassinated the night of his election victory.

The Democratic Party's convention was held in late August in Chicago. For days before the convention, young people gathered to protest the war, the Democratic Party, and things in general. They had many clashes with the Chicago police and the National Guard, who were there in great numbers to keep order. As the convention started, the city was tense.

On the third night of the convention, just as the nominating speeches had begun, a full-scale riot broke out in front of convention headquarters. Many demonstrators, reporters, and bystanders were beaten or assaulted by angry Chicago police. The national TV networks broadcast the action live around the world. Coverage of the convention, which was in near bedlam, was interrupted with coverage of the riot outside. It was a very unpleasant picture of the Democratic Party. Nevertheless, Vice President Humphrey was nominated on the first ballot.

The Democratic Party delegates left Chicago feeling divided, angry, and confused. Public confidence in the ability of the Democrats to govern and to bring peace to Vietnam and the streets at home was very low. Further, the Democrats had picked one of the latest convention dates in modern history, just before Labor Day, to have their convention. They had

Student antiwar protesters clashed with Chicago's police force during the Democratic National Convention. Despite winning the nomination, Humphrey labeled the mayhem—and its negative publicity—a catastrophe.

assumed Lyndon Johnson would be nominated without opposition. The Democrats entered the fall campaign with precious little time to recover.

Nixon, Humphrey, and Wallace appealed to the voters with their proposals. Wallace appeared to be pulling white, conservative but traditionally Democratic voters away from Humphrey. Humphrey distanced himself from Johnson's Vietnam policy and gained ground with liberal McCarthy and Kennedy supporters. Nixon promised an end to the war and the restoration of civil order.

Humphrey and Edmund Muskie *(right)*, his vice-presidential running mate, showed confidence after the Democratic Convention. But the campaign was a three-way contest between Humphrey, Wallace, and former vice president Richard Nixon, who eventually won.

In the end, Nixon won by approximately 31.7 million to 31.2 million for Hubert Humphrey, with 301 electoral votes to Humphrey's 191 electoral votes. Wallace had won about 10 million votes nationwide and had gathered 46 electoral votes. Wallace's candidacy divided voters and took away votes from the Democratic Party's southern base. The three-party race in an emotionally charged atmosphere gave Nixon the win.

ALBERT GORE

(BORN 1948)

THE ELECTION OF 2000

In 2000 President Bill Clinton was finishing his second term. He had won reelection handily in 1996, after defeating President George H. W. Bush, a one-term president, in 1992. The economy grew rapidly during the Clinton years, partly because the yearly federal budget had finally been balanced in the mid-1990s. There was great prosperity, and federal deficits grew into surpluses. There was peace for the United States, except for successful military interventions in Bosnia, Kosovo, and other places. Unfortunately, President Clinton was plagued by several personal scandals during his presidency. The vice president through these triumphs and trying times was Albert Gore Jr.

Gore had served two terms as vice president and before that had served as a senator and congressman for his home state of Tennessee. He was the son of another respected Tennessee senator, Albert Gore Sr. It was expected that the younger Gore would seek the Democratic nomination in 2000.

As the election shaped up, it also became apparent that George W. Bush, the son of George H. W. Bush, would be the Republican candidate. He also came from a powerful political family. He had been governor of Texas since 1994. His father had been the forty-first president, and his grandfather, Prescott Bush, had been a senator from Connecticut.

Despite difficult nomination battles, Bush and Gore won the expected endorsements. Bush promised to push for a massive tax cut, to sponsor

George W. Bush *(center)* **hangs out with his father, President George H. W. Bush** *(right)*, **in Maine.**

educational reform, and to restore integrity to the presidency. Gore promised to continue the era of peace and prosperity achieved under President Clinton. At the same time, he tried to distance himself from the personal scandals of the Clinton administration.

Vice President Gore made history when he chose Senator Joseph Lieberman of Connecticut to run with him as his vice-presidential candidate. Lieberman was the first person of the Jewish religion to be

Al Gore's choice of Joe Lieberman *(right)* **as his vice-presidential running mate was historic. Lieberman was the first Jewish person to run for executive office.**

nominated by a major party for president or vice president. George Bush chose his father's former defense secretary and White House chief of staff Dick Cheney to be the vice-presidential candidate.

By the time of the election in early November, polls showed the candidates to be very close. TV networks were poised to guess the winner. As election evening developed, Gore started showing a slight lead in the popular vote but lagged in the estimated electoral vote. Eventually, the TV electoral map showed Bush winning 31 states and 246 electoral votes and Gore winning 18 states and Washington, D.C., to give him 267 electoral votes. A candidate needed 271 to win.

First, the returns projected Gore the winner, then Bush the winner. Gore conceded to Bush but withdrew the concession when it once again became "too close to call." Only several hundred votes separated Bush from Gore. No winner was announced the day after the election.

The key state was Florida, with its twenty-five electoral votes. The Republicans, led by Florida's governor Jeb Bush, the candidate's brother, thought they could win the state. The Democrats felt that they had a great chance with Senator Lieberman, who could appeal to the state's liberal base and Jewish voters. Under Florida law, with the vote this close, a machine recount was required. This started a protracted and heated legal battle that lasted for several weeks.

Both parties sent scores of attorneys to Florida to fight the legal battles over recounts. Vote recounting went on in various Florida counties. The lower courts rendered various decisions, which were appealed to the Florida Supreme Court. Generally, the Florida Supreme Court's decisions favored the Democrats' request that hand recounting of machine-read ballots must continue.

The Republicans went to federal court to stop the recounting, which would preserve Bush's narrow lead of approximately six hundred votes. Both the Federal District Court and the Circuit

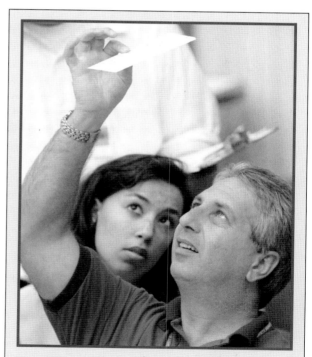

The vote recounting in Florida went on for weeks.

Court of Appeals denied there were any "federal issues." The Florida Supreme Court's decisions were also appealed directly to the U.S. Supreme Court. A central issue in both cases was how much time Florida had to certify its votes. The votes had to be turned in before the Electoral College convened December 18, 2000. As a result, the importance of the Electoral College, the real decision maker, became another issue of debate.

As the Florida lower court and the U.S. Supreme Court moved through the recount and protest procedures, an essential point was Gore's desire to re-count the votes while Bush wanted the recounting to stop. Twice the Florida Supreme Court extended the recount deadline to recount all votes. On December 12, 2000, the U.S. Supreme Court ruled in Bush's favor, stopping the recounting of votes in Florida. Gore conceded the closest electoral defeat in history, 271 to 267.

FEDERAL LAW REQUIRES THAT ALL CONTROVERSIES

about state election counts must be resolved at least six days (by December 12) before the meeting of the electors (on December 18). In 2000 the U.S. Supreme Court was worried that the recount would not end before the meeting of electors on December 18 and also that standards for judging votes might differ in various precincts. As a result, the court cut off the recount ordered by the Florida Supreme Court. On January 3, 2001, the electoral votes were counted by hand in Congress and the results announced by Vice President Gore, as presiding officer of the Senate. Bush won the electoral vote 271 to 267 and was inaugurated on January 20, 2001.

The Florida recount continued for more than five weeks after Election Day. It was the most watched elective contest in the nation's history. Even though Gore had won the popular vote by more than six hundred thousand votes, George W. Bush became the next president.

Voters show their support for George W. Bush in the 2000 election recount. One marcher is dressed as a "chad," the part of the ballot that is punched out to show a person's vote. Chads that had not been completely punched out contributed to the long recounting process and to voter confusion on the election's outcome.

The most important facet of the 2000 election was that it proved again that the rule of law provides an orderly transfer of power. This is surely the essence of American strength. Given the passions and fervor of both sides of this election, the fact that an orderly process was used to reach a decision was highly significant. The peaceful transfer of the immense power of the presidency without violence or the use of military force is a tribute to our democracy and to the Constitution, which is its foundation. The value of our freedoms and democratic institutions was reaffirmed, and our appreciation for these institutions was renewed.

IF NEITHER CANDIDATE HAD RECEIVED 271

electoral votes in the Electoral College, what would have happened?

In an unprecedented move, the justices of the U.S. Supreme Court decided the 2000 election.

The electoral decision would have gone to the House of Representatives, as it had in 1800 and 1824. The House votes by state delegation, not by party. Because Bush had won the popular votes in the majority of states, he would have won a majority of states' votes and thus the election. However, the U.S. Supreme Court intervened and awarded Florida's electoral votes to George W. Bush.

The U.S. Supreme Court's involvement in the case was unprecedented. Its decision to stop the voting recount was an equally unprecedented involvement in politics. The court's five to four decision was on politically partisan lines. All five justices voting to support Bush's position were Republican appointees. Among the four dissenters, two were Democratic nominees and two were Republicans.

BIBLIOGRAPHY

Congressional Quarterly, Inc. *Presidential Elections 1789–1996*. Washington, DC: Congressional Quarterly, Inc., 1997.

Cook, Rhodes. *Race for the Presidency: Winning the 2000 Nomination*. Washington, DC: CQ Press, 2000.

"Henry Clay." *Encyclopaedia Britannica*. Vol. 5. Chicago: Encyclopaedia Britannica, Inc., 1973.

Minneapolis StarTribune, November–December 2000.

Scammon, Richard H., Alice V. McGilivray, and Rhodes Cook. *America Votes 24: A Handbook of Contemporary American Election Statistics*. Washington, DC: CQ Press, 2001.

"United States of America." *Encyclopaedia Britannica*. Vol. 24. Chicago: Encyclopaedia Britannica, Inc., 1973.

Wall Street Journal, November–December 2000.

FURTHER READING AND WEBSITES

BOOKS

Barber, James G. *Eyewitness: Presidents*. New York: DK Publishing, 2000.

Bausum, Ann. *Our Country's Presidents*. Washington, DC: National Geographic Society, 2001.

Cleveland, Will. *Yo, Millard Fillmore: And All Those Presidents You Don't Know*. New Milford, CT: Millbrook, 1997.

Donovan, Sandy. *Running for Office: A Look at Political Campaigns*. Minneapolis: Lerner Publications Company, 2004.

Fish Durost, Bruce, and Becky Fish Durost. *The History of the Democratic Party*. Broomall, PA: Chelsea House, 1999.

Kronenwetter, Michael. *Political Parties of the United States*. Berkeley Heights, NJ: Enslow, 1996.

Landau, Elaine. *Friendly Foes: A Look at Political Parties*. Minneapolis: Lerner Publications Company, 2004.

————. *The President's Work: A Look at the Executive Branch*. Minneapolis: Lerner Publications Company, 2004.

————. *2000 Presidential Election*. New York: Scholastic Library Publishing, 2001.

Lutz, Norma Jean. *The History of the Republican Party*. Broomall, PA: Chelsea House, 2000.

Márquez, Herón. *George W. Bush*. Minneapolis: Lerner Publications Company, 2002.

———. *Richard M. Nixon*. Minneapolis: Lerner Publications Company, 2002.

Morin, Isobel. V. *Politics, American Style: Political Parties in American History*. Brookfield, CT: Twenty-First Century Books, 1999.

Roberts, Jeremy. *Franklin D. Roosevelt*. Minneapolis: Lerner Publications Company, 2002.

Sandler, Martin W. *Presidents*. New York: HarperCollins, 1995.

St. George, Judith. *So You Want to Be President?* East Rutherford, NJ: Philomel Books, 2000.

Sullivan, George. *Choosing the Candidates*. Englewood Cliffs, NJ: Silver Burdett, 1991.

WEBSITES

Ben's Guide to U.S. Government for Kids
<http://www.bensguide.gpo.gov>
Follow Ben Franklin through the various levels of the U.S. government with this fun and interactive website. Divided into four age levels, the site provides information that kids of all ages can understand.

FirstGov for Kids
<http://www.kids.gov/k_gov.htm>
FirstGov for Kids is a great resource site that provides links to individual, state-maintained sites, as well as kid-friendly sites that deal with the U.S. government.

The History of Political Parties
<www.americanhistory.about.com/cs/politicalparties/>
This website offers a look at past and present political parties of the United States.

Life at the Conventions—1948–1996
<www.lifemag.com/life/conventions>
Enjoy this web gallery of photos that captures the excitement of political conventions in the twentieth century.

The PBS Kids Democracy Project
<www.pbs.org/democracy/kids/educators>
This websites offers information on what government does and why we need government.

United States Presidents
<http://www.kidsnewsroom.com/elmer/infocentral/frameset/presidents/>
Stop here for a brief biography of the presidents of the United States. While you're here, match presidents with their vice presidents.

INDEX

ABOUT THE AUTHOR

David J. Goldman is an attorney practicing in Minneapolis, Minnesota. He received his bachelor's degree in journalism and his law degree from the University of Minnesota, where he also studied American history as a graduate student.

PHOTO ACKNOWLEDGMENTS

Photographs are reproduced with the permission of: © Reuters NewMedia, Inc./CORBIS, pp. 7, 64, 65, 67; Collection of the New Jersey Historical Society, Newark, New Jersey, p. 9; © Bettmann/CORBIS, pp. 11, 47, 59, 60; Library of Congress, pp. 12, 14, 17, 18, 19, 21, 23, 24, 28 (both), 32, 33, 34, 41, 46; The New York Public Library, p. 13; Virginia State Library, p. 15; United States Army, pp. 20, 56; Dictionary of American Portraits, pp. 26, 27; Rutherford B. Hayes Library, p. 30; Chicago Historical Society, p. 31; Professional Picture Service, p. 35; Tennessee State Library and Archives, p. 36; Kansas State Historical Society, Topeka, Kansas, p. 38; Franklin D. Roosevelt Library, p. 39; Independent Picture Service, pp. 40, 43; New York Historical Society, p. 42; Illustrated London News, p. 45; Illinois State Historical Library, p. 48; Associated Press, *Flint Journal*, p. 49; National Museum of American History, Smithsonian Institution, p. 50; Minnesota Historical Society, p. 51; United Press International, pp. 52, 57; United Nations, p. 53; Office of Senator Humphrey, p. 54; National Archives, pp. 55, 58; Southdale-Hennepin Area Library, p. 61; Clinton/Gore National Campaign Headquarters, p. 62; George Bush Presidential Library, p. 63; The Supreme Court Historical Society, p. 68. Cartoons on cover and chapter openers by Bill Hauser.